SCHOOLS FOR STRATEGY:
TEACHING STRATEGY FOR 21ST CENTURY CONFLICT

Colin S. Gray

November 2009

*****

*****

Comments pertaining to this report are invited and should be forwarded to: Director, Strategic Studies Institute, U.S. Army War College, 122 Forbes Ave, Carlisle, PA 17013-5244.

*****

This manuscript was funded by the U.S. Army War College External Research Associates Program. Information on this program is available on our website, *www.StrategicStudiesInstitute. army.mil*, at the Publishing button.

*****

ISBN 978-1-257-13177-8

FOREWORD

Education in strategy is feasible and important. Few are the would-be strategists who are beyond improvement by some formal education. However, for such education to be well directed, it needs to rest upon sound assumptions concerning the eternal nature, meaning, and function, yet ever shifting character of strategy, and the range of behaviors required for effective strategic performance. This monograph strives to shed light on these fundamental matters.

Dr. Gray emphasizes the necessity for strategic education to help develop the strategic approach, the way of thinking that can solve or illuminate strategic problems. He advises that such education should not strive for a spurious relevance by presenting a military variant of current affairs. Also, the strategist will perform better for today if he has mastered and can employ strategy's general theory.

The monograph is relatively optimistic, in that it argues the case for strategy being both possible and, in some helpful measure, teachable.

DOUGLAS C. LOVELACE, JR.
Director
Strategic Studies Institute

iii

ABOUT THE AUTHOR

COLIN S. GRAY is Professor of International Politics and Strategic Studies at the University of Reading, England. He worked at the International Institute for Strategic Studies (London), and at Hudson Institute (Croton-on-Hudson, NY) before founding the National Institute for Public Policy, a defense-oriented think tank in the Washington, DC, area. Dr. Gray served for 5 years in the Reagan administration on the President's General Advisory Committee on Arms Control and Disarmament. He has served as an adviser to both the U.S. and British governments (he has dual citizenship). His government work has included studies of nuclear strategy, arms control, maritime strategy, space strategy, and the use of special forces. Dr. Gray has written 23 books, including: *The Sheriff: America's Defense of the New World Order* (University Press of Kentucky, 2004); *Another Bloody Century: Future Warfare* (Weidenfeld and Nicolson, 2005); *Strategy and History: Essays on Theory and Practice* (Routledge, 2006); *War, Peace, and International Relations: An Introduction to Strategic History* (Routledge, 2007; Potomac Books, 2009); and *National Security Dilemmas: Challenges and Opportunities* (Potomac Books, 2009). His next book is *The Strategy Bridge: Theory for Practice* (Oxford University Press, forthcoming). Currently, he is researching and writing a book on the theory and practice of airpower. Dr. Gray is a graduate of the Universities of Manchester and Oxford.

SUMMARY

Because strategic performance must involve the ability to decide, to command, and to lead, as well as the capacity to understand, there are practical limits to what is feasible and useful by way of formal education in strategy. The soldier who best comprehends what Sun-tzu, Clausewitz, and Thucydides intended to say, is not necessarily the soldier best fitted to strategic high command. It is important to distinguish between intellect and character/personality. The superior strategist is ever uniquely a product of nature/biology, personality/psychology, and experience/opportunity. Nonetheless, formal education has its place.

Strategic genius is rare, strategic talent is more common, though still unusual. The latter can be improved by formal education, the former most probably cannot. However, there is merit in the educational aspiration to help educate instinct for a better performance.

It is fortunate that genius is not strictly required in our strategists since education is apt to be unable to reach it. What we do require is competence based on a talent that can be educated. There is no denying that because strategy is a pragmatic creative activity, the strategist—well-educated or not in a formal sense—ideally has to know what to do, how to do it, and, last but not least, he/she needs to be able to do it. Obviously, biology and psychology shaped by the opportunities granted by experience loom large here. Professors of Strategy cannot so teach their military students that they are truly fit for purpose as strategists-in-action. But professors can help educate the strategic judgment of those soldiers and civilians who are educable.

Because it is a practical real-world endeavor, strategy and its strategists do not have to secure a grade of excellence, though that certainly is right as the ambition. By its very nature, our strategy has to be good enough to compete with the enemy's strategy, in the whole strategic context. By that, I mean that even if strategy is relatively uninspired, so complex is competition and war that fungibility may save us. Our generals, or troops, or equipment, or tactics might be less than stellar, but somewhere amidst the myriad facets of statecraft, war, and warfare, we might be able to locate and exploit compensating advantages.

Although the classroom (of several kinds) cannot put in what God and nature omitted, it does not follow that strategy cannot be taught to good effect. Any strategically educable person should have their capacity for sound and perhaps superior strategic judgment improved by intense exposure to the small canon of classic texts on general strategic theory. Even though personal experience is the finest teacher, there should be no denying the value in consideration of the wisdom distilled from lifelong learning by the greatest strategic minds of all time. If one is unable to profit as a strategist from careful study of Sun-tzu, Thucydides, Clausewitz, and Edward N. Luttwak, then one should not aspire to the strategic baton—unless one truly is a genius, of course.

The strategic educator seeks to assist the student in his ability to think strategically. He has to help hone performance of the strategic function which obligates a coherent meshing of ends, ways, and means. All too often it is popular to teach strategy only with empirical reference to our contemporary and anticipated near-future challenges. This is understandable but nonetheless is an error. Strategic studies worthy of the name can degenerate into a professionally narrowly competent variant of current affairs. The students initially value what they see as high personal relevance in the strategic problems of today, but that very relevance is likely to shape and bias their analysis. Because strategy and its function is eternal and universal, there is much to be said for taking students out of their contemporary comfort zone of familiar detail and instead obliging them to reason strategically for different times and places. The basic problems will be discovered to be startlingly similar. The strategic educator does not seek to develop experts on the strategic issues of the early 21st century. Rather he strives to educate aspiring strategists in the ability to think strategically and exercise strategic judgment.

Indispensable to an education in strategy is recognition of strategy's limits. Strategic performance requires a tactical competence by its sword arm that it cannot always assume. Similarly, and as much to the point, the prospects for a superior strategic performance must be impacted massively by the wisdom or otherwise in the politics-as-policy that turns the official key for action and propels it. The strategist has to devise and execute plans (theories) for military behavior that should advance and perhaps secure the goals specified by policy. But those goals can be ill chosen, and they vary with political mood and circumstance. It is the duty of the strategist to try to match purposeful military effort and its consequences with the country's political interests expressed as policy. This can be a mission of heroic difficulty, even to the point of impossibility.

One reason why strategic performance can be poor is because senior military strategists may prove unable to communicate effectively on military realities to professional politicians who do not want to be told what most probably cannot be done, and therefore should not be attempted. While it is the duty of policy to listen to, and conduct genuine dialog with military expertise, it is the duty of the military profession so to educate its senior strategists that such a dialog worthy of the name is possible. A well-educated strategist is a person who is educated in more than strategy. A liberal education in the classical sense must be helpful to the human performance that is a key enabler of high quality in national strategic performance.

SCHOOLS FOR STRATEGY: TEACHING STRATEGY FOR 21ST CENTURY CONFLICT

Caesar was a soldiers' general, but he thought beyond his soldiers. Here the matter may be left. The art of war under the Roman Republic was something that belonged at Rome, a plant that grew in Roman soil, something which needed for its application talent not genius, but in its culmination, it did produce a soldier greater than itself, a soldier in whom there was that fusing together of intellect and will that marks off genius from talent [i.e., Caesar].

F. E. Adcock, 1940[1]

In a 1973 book on grand strategy, defense specialist John Collins observed that while "strategy is a game that anyone can play, it is not a game that just anyone can play well. Only the most gifted participants have much chance to win a prize...."

Individuals either have the cognitive skills for strategy or they do not, and Collins' observation, based on years of experience with National War College graduates, is most do not—not even among field-grade military officers with the potential for flag rank. There is scant evidence to date that professional education or training are at all successful in inculcating strategic insight into most individuals. Instead, the best we can do is to try to identify those individuals who have this talent and then make sure that they are put in positions in which they can use it to good effect.

Andrew F. Krepinevich and
Barry D. Watts, 2009;
John Collins, 1973[2]

Introduction: Issues.

The difference between talent and genius is the difference between, respectively, Dwight D. Eisenhower and Omar Bradley on the one hand, and George S. Patton on the other. An education in strategy cannot close the gap between the two categories, no matter what theory for tailored improvement is favored. No syllabus, theoretical or practical, can insert what God and biology fail to provide. So much for some of the bad news. The better news is that talent typically is good enough to get the strategy job done. This talent needs only to be sufficient to outstrategize the enemy's strategist(s), always assuming that the villain of the day does not enjoy some major structural advantage in conflict. If that should be the case, then one has need of superior strategic skill, indeed possibly of genius, to offset (and more) the unfriendly material, or other, imbalance. The Thirteen Colonies needed superior strategy, as did the Confederate States of America. The former were suitably blessed, the latter were well blessed, but insufficiently so. It should be needless to add that the quality of strategy one requires depends nontrivially upon the quality and quantity of the enemy as adaptive competitor in purposeful violence. In John Collins' apt words, "[s]trategy is not a game that states can play by themselves."[3]

There are nearly always severe problems with strategic genius, and the downside, alas, is inseparable from the upside. The qualities that make vitally for genius in a strategist are, unfortunately, supported and possibly even enabled by such undesirable characteristics of personality as a monstrously large ego, intolerance of criticism, a problem with delegation, a thoroughly self-regarding life-style, a gigantic ambition, and a tendency to overconfidence. These are heavy burdens for genius to bear, but some or all of them are virtually unavoidable if genius is permitted to do its thing. It is almost unnecessary to mention that strategic genius, cursed inalienably with the potent virus that matures into the Great Person Syndrome, understandably is found offensive by career would-be rivals, as well as by the unfortunates who have to service the often extraordinary habits of the Great Person in question.

The epigraphs and opening paragraphs to this monograph have emphasized the all too human dimension to strategy. Our subject may be the teaching of strategy, but history and logic both should be allowed to tell us that bringing horses to water guarantees neither that they will drink, nor that they will be able to benefit adequately even if they do. The epigraphs were chosen because they highlight master themes for this narrative. They claim that strategic talent can be distinguished from strategic genius; that strategic genius is exceedingly rare; and that even mere competence in strategy, simply some talent, is unusual. Plainly, on these summary assessments, strategy is strictly a super-elite set of behaviors accessible for performance only by few people. This is probably true, at least it sounds plausible. Whether or not this plausible claim can withstand critical scrutiny remains to be determined. Moreover, it may prove to be the case that strategic genius and strategic competence comprise well enough a linear spectrum, not two distinct categories rigidly separated by a chasm that enforces discontinuity. Genius overall, in common with the physical and moral courage of which it is partially made, may sensibly be seen to be episodic rather than systematically permanent. In other words, genius can have a bad day, or at least an off day when it is merely competent, or occasionally much worse. For example, there can be little doubt that Lee was not at his best on Day 3 at Gettysburg, while Napoleon demonstrated scant excellence in generalship on the day of the battle at Waterloo.[4]

Although we must discuss the substance of strategy, what it is that should be taught, it is no less important that we consider the students of strategic education: Who are they? What do they need to be able to do? What can, and what most probably can they not, be taught? A discussion like this has no merit, in fact it can only confuse, if the key terms are not defined early and employed subsequently with consistency. Unfortunately, few subjects of deep concern to the U.S. defense community are harassed by so much misunderstanding as is debate over all matters deemed "strategic." This monograph, therefore, must begin with clarification of the conceptual fundamentals. Subsequently, the story arc proceeds to consider the historical context for strategy in the 21st century; approaches to the teaching of strategy; and the desirable content of strategic education. The initial step in the journey has to be specification of exactly what is, and is not, encompassed by the concept of strategy, and just what does, and what does not, warrant qualification by the powerful adjective, "strategic."

The Nature and Character of Strategy: Fundamentals.

It is noticeable how often a profound understanding of a subject is advanced by trinitarian theorizing. The deepest of Thucydides' compound insights unarguably is his identification of the prime motives

4

both in decisions for war and in statecraft broadly in the oft-quoted triptych of "fear, honor, and interest."[5] Carl von Clausewitz corralled his somewhat rebellious ingredients of war into his preferred "wondrous trinity," consisting of passion and violence; chance, opportunity, and uncertainty; and reason in policy.[6] Properly approached, strategy needs to be understood within the triadic framework of ends, ways, and means. However, the actual complex balance of relative weight among the three fundamental elements of strategy will vary hugely from occasion to occasion.

Lest readers regard this section of the monograph as an academician's diversion from the real subject, I must hasten to explain that confusion over concepts, functions, and the relationships among them, can render efforts at strategic education more harmful than beneficial. The medical rule, "first, do no harm," applies amply to well-intentioned efforts at education in strategy. The guiding light for this analysis is provided, as so often is the case, by Clausewitz. The Prussian wrote that "[t]he primary purpose of any theory is to clarify concepts and ideas that have become, as it were, confused and entangled."[7]

The words that we employ matter profoundly because they shape the way that we are able to think about phenomena. As we shall strive to explain, because there are more than enough causes of poor strategic performance over which the strategist has only limited control, if that, there should be no excuse for self-inflicted, hence gratuitous, conceptual wounds. For the scholar, definitions are arbitrary, discretionary, ever arguable, and are judged more or less useful, which is to say fit for their purpose. Warriors, of course, do not enjoy the luxury of scholarly discretion over the common meaning of words and phrases. Manuals of doctrine have to define terms to ensure that all users employ the same words with the same meanings. Since this monograph is not a venture in doctrine creation, it limits its ambition to the attempt at clarity in explanation, with precise choice of words accorded only a secondary significance, always provided the language does not impede the explanation.

It has long been commonplace to claim that while one *has* a strategy, one *does* tactics. This is useful, and in an important sense true, but, alas, it is also misleading. Why is that so? The truth that strategy is done by tactics is overshadowed by the yet greater truth that strategy is done as tactics.

Wayne P. Hughes, Jr., advises wisely that:

> At the most fundamental level, it is accepted that the strategist directs the tactician. The mission of every battle plan is passed from the higher commander to the lower. There is no more basic precept than that, and no principle of war is given greater status than the primacy of the objective.
>
> This is not the same as saying that strategy determines tactics and the course of battle. Strategy and tactics are best thought of as handmaidens, but if one must choose, it is probably more correct to say that tactics come first because they dictate the limits of strategy. Strategy must be conceived with battle in mind. . . .[8]

There is a crucial sense in which tactical behavior cannot help to be other than strategic behavior. It may be paradoxical, but it is really inescapable, that theory (strategy as a plan) and practice (tactical action) are one, they comprise a *gestalt*. The paradox arises in the inalienable and simultaneous essential unity of strategy and tactics, and their no less essential and inalienable difference. The difference is that between

6

purpose and instrument. In principle, tactical behavior should not be strictly self-referential, as it were autistic, because then it must lack the very political meaning that defines it as warfare in war. In these pages, I shall advance the thesis that both the theory and the practice of strategy need to be taught, insofar as they can be, because an education in strategy must encompass ideas and the application of those ideas as plans that have to be implemented by command performance. All of the "dots" need to be connected, from strategy's general theory to the tactical doing of a strategy at any and every level of warfare, in any and every kind of war.[9]

Unarguably, the meaning of the word strategy has altered, by and large it has become ever more inclusive up the logical and command hierarchy, since the late 18th century. Scholars can argue and have argued about the linguistic provenance of our contemporary usage of the word.[10] What matters is that we should not confuse ourselves, and that we should be inoculated by sound strategic education against false doctrines, faddish concepts, ephemerally fashionable buzzwords, and the chaotic and inconsistent (mis)use of language. Any definition of strategy unambiguously must convey the idea that it is about directing and using something to achieve a selected purpose. Extant definitions abound, and many of them have a distinctive merit. For the purpose of this discussion for the intended audience for this monograph, I choose to define (military) strategy as *the direction and use that is made of force and the threat of force for the ends of policy*. Deliberately following, but not slavishly repeating, Clausewitz, I distinguish as clearly as I am able between (military) assets and the use that is made of them. *On War* provides the verbal formula: "[s]trategy is the use of the engagement for the purpose of the war."[11] It proceeds immediately to explain that "[t]he strategist must therefore define an aim for the entire operational side of the war that will be in accordance with its purpose. In other words, he will draft the plan of the war." Emphatically, Clausewitz does not say, or mean, that tactics is what happens in the battlespace, be the geography extensive or confined, while strategy is what is done away from that battlespace. He does not confuse strategy with logistics.

Instrumentality is the most core of the ideas that express the nature of strategy. It is the purposeful use of some instrument or instruments. That purpose, whatever it may be — political in the case in point here — can be achieved in whole or in part only by the securing of some control over the rival/enemy.[12] And the pursuit of such control is performed with a plan, a strategy. The plan can be formal or informal, rigid or flexible, well conceived or otherwise, developed by an elaborate process of staffwork and consultation among stakeholders, or by a lonely individual, but plan there should be. Ironically, strategic effect is generated whether or not there is anything that resembles a strategy in a plan. All military (tactical) behavior has strategic weight, be it ever so small or even of net negative value.[13] To explain: The course of events in a conflict is shaped in good part by competing military performances. Those interlocking and somewhat interdependent military performances will happen, and will have consequences, military and political, whether or not the belligerents did strategy explicitly. In practice, all belligerents cannot help but do strategy by default, even should the strategic function be seriously undergoverned or even absent altogether as a cohesive and purposeful whole endeavor.

Some experienced intending reformers of the American Professional Military Education (PME) have noted plausibly that strategy is neither arcane and mysterious, nor is it confined to a particular level of war, that is, above operations and below policy. Instead, they claim credibly enough that the strategic function is authoritative at every level, and that strategy can and should be taught with this in mind.[14] What they mean, correctly in this educator's opinion, is that all players in the national security hierarchy must do, or contribute somehow to the doing, of strategy, for their particular purposes. Clarified, this translates as the thesis that the trinity of ends, ways, and means, or should it be ends, means, and ways for interesting variation, explain what is attempted in tactics, operations, military strategy, and grand strategy. Every soldier with some command responsibility, great or small, has to manage this inescapable trinity of factors as best he can.

Unfortunately for the would-be strategic educator, the elegant simplicity of the concept of a triadically structured strategic function working at every level is entirely too simple, notwithstanding its essential truth. The challenge is two-fold and complex. First, is it necessary but not sufficient for the tactical soldier to understand how his available means can best be employed to achieve the objectives he is given. That alone is no easy matter. In addition, the tactical and operational (level) soldier requires some grasp of at least the realities at the next level above his responsibilities. The tactician needs to know the operational purpose of his tactical behavior, lest the latter harm the former. Similarly, the operational level soldier, the general, has to comprehend why his selected behavior should advance the prospects for success overall in the course of the war. As Robert Lyman claims convincingly, the operational level of warfare needs to be conducted by generals who have a "strategic sense."[15] But there is a long tradition of belief that the operational level of warfare is one wherein classic generalship can be exercised in a military context that is blessedly politics-free, or at least politics-lite. This is a perilously erroneous belief.

The second major problem with the neatly functional-at-every-level view of strategy, is the challenge of currency conversion in the absence of a stable exchange rate. This challenge grows mightily in difficulty as one ascends the pertinent hierarchy from tactics through operations, to military strategy, grand strategy, and policy, all the way to the inspiring vision which launched and then fuelled it all with probably vague higher purpose (a single communized world community, a very much greater Germany, a wholly democratized, "free," and free-standing, community of states, and the like).[16] With respect to relative quality of trouble, the most difficult challenge is that posed to the military strategist who must, with military effects and their consequences, change currency from net military achievement to net political result. It is one thing to estimate the character and weight of aerial bombardment necessary to secure some specific level of damage. It is quite another to seek to identify metrically a cause and effect nexus between damage imposed and enemy political compliance.[17] I must rush to add that even the relatively easy task, that of prediction of damage, let alone the military and economic harm that that should impose, is a far from elementary task. The point of emphasis here is that although the strategic function must apply to all levels of warfare and war, the heart of the matter, and necessarily the focus of this monograph, has to be the mission of education on strategic effect where military achievement has to count in the foreign currency of political will. Clausewitz was in no doubt as to the scale of the challenge. The generically strategic (ends-ways-means) problem may seem to be wholly military for the tactician and the operational level soldier, but this is not so. *On War* enlightens as follows:

> If you want to overcome your enemy, you must match your effort against his power of resistance, which can be expressed as the product of two inseparable factors, viz. *the total means at his disposal* and *the strength of his will*. The extent of the means at his disposal is a matter – though not exclusively – of figures, and should be measurable. But the strength of his will is much less easy to determine and can only be gauged approximately by the strength of the motive animating it.[18]

In seeking to understand strategy, it is necessary to recognize that it is locatable diagrammatically on a horizontal as well as a vertical axis of implied relative authority. This claim means that although strategy is logically and even officially typically placed between policy and tactics (to simplify), there is a vital sense in which the interdependence among the three – yet another crucial threesome – is perilously underrated by the hierarchical model.[19] The flow chart showing ideal connections, with descending authority and domain, yet with helpful feedback(up) loops, quite often bears no relationship to actual historical practice. To illustrate, if for now your army cannot win decisive success by fighting (tactically), you are obliged to adopt a long-haul strategy guided by a concept of victory by attrition. Tactics can dictate strategy, at least they can if policy dictates to the army that it must achieve a complete military victory. This illustrative logic was the actual condition of the land warfare in World War I from 1915 until the late Summer of 1918. The true villains of the piece were the politicians on both sides who demanded more of their armies than those armies could deliver. Tactical feasibility drove strategic choice. This is an enduring fact about warfare. Strategic success has to be forged from tactical advantage. If the latter is unattainable, for whatever blend of reasons, then strategy is mere vain ambition.

Why do we want to teach strategy for 21st century conflict? Obviously, the answer has to be because we need strategists to do strategy for us. But, who are they? What are their roles? And what, exactly, do we mean by "doing strategy"? For easily understandable reasons, academics are prone to a preference for teaching strategy on a curriculum that privileges ideas. The widespread recognition of the fortunate existence of one or two handfuls — recently I have specified 10 — of authors of classic works of strategy theory, has the somewhat unfortunate consequence of encouraging overemphasis upon intellectual potency at the cost of character and personality.[20] Modern works on strategy, especially those written by a civilian (such as this author), readily can mislead an unduly credulous readership into believing that the key to strategic competence is conceptual grasp. Such grasp is indeed essential. It is necessary that would-be strategists be assisted in their, in fact, our, effort to know how to think about strategy. But mastery of the theory of strategy, even when the theory is appreciated courtesy of the finest thoughts by the sharpest minds in strategic intellectual history, is not synonymous with mastery of strategy. Michael Clarke explained in a pithy maxim that "[i]t is easy to think strategically, it is hard to act strategically."[21] The first half of the dictum is eminently challengeable, but the second, in juxtaposition with the first, offers close to brilliant insight, notwithstanding its apparent banality. I am concerned that this monograph of teaching strategy should corral properly its true components. If we can assume, as we should, that strategy, even strategic theory or thinking—following Bernard Brodie—is a pragmatic subject, we can contextualize suitably the intellectual dimension to strategic education.[22] Rephrased, we need to answer the elementary, nay elemental, question, "What are we educating aspiring strategists for?" In order to answer that question, we have to answer the prior one, "What might strategists need to be able to do?" What does it mean to be a "strategist"? I suggest that a strategist could be required, within the meaning of "strategist," to:

1. Theorize abstractly and contribute to the development, or more accurately the interpretation, of strategy's eternal and universal general theory.

2. Conceive, invent, or discover, the master idea(s) that provide the basic guidance for planners in particular historical contexts.

3. Shape and draft the actual historical operational plans, also known as strategies, for the use of the armed forces; this requires command and control of the process of strategic planning, including adaptive planning once the enemy begins to cast his vote.

4. Command and control of the attempted implementation of plans by troops "in the field," a broad duty that entails choice of subordinate commanders, overwatch of their performance, and, to repeat, readiness to adjust plans as events unfold. Classic generalship is necessary at several levels of responsibility, involving command and leadership.

This typology is only a rather foreshortened shortlist. It would be plausible to claim some need for the "strategist" to be able to function at one end of the spectrum as a politician; while at the other end, we may have some requirement for the aura of heroic warrior. The important point is that the teaching of strategy cannot be divorced from an intelligent understanding of the full range of the strategist's possible roles. The central truth here is that strategy is an applied scientific art, with emphasis mainly on the noun and not the adjective. Strategy cannot sensibly be regarded and treated pedagogically as if it were a free-floating body of mighty truths. It is not a cluster of brilliant insights mined from the depths of Thucydides, Sun-tzu, and Clausewitz, although the products of such mining, properly contextualized, indeed is essential for an education in strategy pedagogically worthy of the name. Strategic theory is only entertainment, even a source of ironic amusement, save with reference to its value for strategic practice. And, to reemphasize, strategic practice cannot strictly be defined as the cogitations, or even the activities of planning and commanding performed by people designated offi-cially as strategists. The reason, to repeat, is because all military activity has some net strategic weight that scores for the home team on the course of events. Every corporal is a strategic corporal. Also, recall the claim advanced earlier that the strategic function of mutually adjusting for coherence the eternal elements of ends, ways, and means, is a feature of all levels of military behavior in warfare.[23]

To ensure that this discussion does not lose focus because of the desire of the author-theorist to be comprehensive and logically rigorous, as well as faith-ful to historical reality, it is time for me to narrow the aim of the analysis. For the purposes of this monograph, a strategist is understood to be a professional military person charged either, or both, with: (1) guiding and shaping subordinate military operations by major units in campaigns for the purpose of securing military advantage (success or victory); and (2) guiding and shaping the course of military events for the purpose of achieving the polity's political goals. In short, the subject of primary interest here is education for generals coping down the chain of command with the use of major military formations, and for generals striving to deliver upwards for the satisfaction of policy the military advantage achieved by the operational level of warfare. I am aware of the historical fact that in different times, places, and circumstances, the relations among politics, strategy, and tactics can assume widely different forms. Nonetheless, the two core behaviors just identified as our prime foci, truly are ubiquitous in kind. All belligerents have to strive for purposeful coherence in the activities by the elements that contribute to their military instrument; and all belligerents, similarly, must seek to employ that instrument in such ways that their political ambitions are advanced. The strategic function is eternal, looking both up and down the vertical hierarchy. It may be anachronistic to employ such words as strategy and grand strategy when we seek to recover the motives of, say, Roman and Byzantine politicians and military commanders. But, some historians' views in opposition notwithstanding, the Romans "did" strategy and grand strategy.[24] This is not to dismiss the charge of anachronism quite out of hand too peremptorily. The accusation of inappropriate backward projection of our contemporary concepts upon Romans, *inter alia*, who were innocent of our words, does have some small merit. Anachronism can have value.

It is useful to return to the important subject of what it is that we require of our strategists, grand and, especially significant for this monograph, military. For what and in what do we need to educate strategists? Norman F. Dixon's seriously flawed classic *On the Psychology of Military Incompetence* made at least one highly significant, verifiably accurate, broad judgment that is helpful for our enquiry.[25] Specifically, he insisted plausibly that the principal cause of military incompetence was not stupidity. Dixon was impressed by the rigidity, the stubbornness, of some commanders. In trying to bring psychology to the task of understanding why some commanders succeed and then fail, the professional psychologist tends to bring too much potential help to the job to be useful. For a leading example, the concept of the authoritarian personality has a way of overdetermining what in truth is a challenge to comprehension that should be met neither by one or two imperial hypotheses, nor by a dominant approach, in this case psychology. Psychohistory offers only one window into a person, and a noticeably unreliable one at that.

Psychologists are right to insist upon the significance of personality for behavior, but in common with most professions, they tend to provide only a single tool for a problem-set with features that defy investigation along only one track. The endeavor to educate strategists has to be shaped with a clear-eyed view of what makes for competence or better, or the opposite, in a person whose job description fits the rather exclusive definition offered here. Education in strategy is seeking to influence a person whose performance must be the dynamic product of the mixture of biology, psychology/personality, experience, and opportunity. Intellect alone is not the key to high strategic performance. It may suffice if the strategist must perform strictly as a planner, though even then an individual will need to be effective in communicating the fruits of his brilliance to others for the common good of the excellent plan. Character cannot substitute for intelligence, but neither can a high IQ stand duty for personality features necessary for leadership, if not always for command.

The brightest students at service academies do not always make superior strategists. The most effective tactical leaders may not shine at higher levels of command. Recall the infamous "Peter Principle," that people rise to their level of incompetence. Sometimes, excellent colonels are promoted to be adequate brigadier generals, and then to be dangerously incompetent major and lieutenant generals. No less interesting, lackluster junior officers, if they can survive through the promotion process, have been known to deliver ever improving performance with each step up in rank. There is no reliable correlation, let alone certain cause and effect, between effectiveness in doing strategy tactically (if I may be excused the apparent oxymoron), and thinking, planning, and commanding tactical success for more inclusive gains. Bluntly stated, good tacticians do not always prove to be good strategists; while good strategists need not have recorded a truly glittering career at the tactical level of warfare. But it is a general rule of no little authority that a person who might become a famously first-class strategist will never be granted the opportunity to shine at that higher level unless first he can perform well enough at those lower ranks wherein the duties did not fit his capabilities so closely. There is irony in the probable fact that some of the qualities that contribute usefully to career success, and which seem plainly to point the way eventually (accidents and enemies permitting) to many "stars," are probably features either irrelevant, or even harmful, to genuinely strategic performance.

The relevance of these paragraphs to this narrative lies in their contribution to an understanding of the human dimension to the challenge of teaching strategy. Also, scarcely less important, they help maintain focus upon "the plot," which should be an inclusive approach to performance of the strategic function. Armed forces have no interest in strategic concepts per se. They need mastery of strategic concepts tied together as coherent theory, because strategy has to be done by strategists on top of their subject. And, it should be needless to repeat for a military readership, the strategic ideas that are adapted for particular needs in plans then have to be translated into action "in the battlespace," guided adaptively by military command and sufficient control. A civilian university can attempt erroneously to teach strategic theory solely with reference to intellectual history. But soldiers must use theory for their practice. And the practice of strategy calls for qualities of character that extend beyond, though assuredly include, the intellect. If moral courage of a high order and at least a good intellect are not both present, the outcome is apt to be the courageously determined, stubborn pursuit of a foolish plan, or — for a variant — the inability to decide which among several exciting and creative options to pursue, or perhaps a lack of courage to match the brilliance of a strategic operational conception.

Civilian scholars have been known to have trouble really understanding the second half of the quotation offered from Michael Clarke (page 12). For the soldier, and by extension for the policymaker who has to depend upon the soldier, theory and practice must be approached holistically. The United States requires not only colonels and generals to understand strategy, vital though that is, no less it needs generals who can get the core job of successful combat done in the field. This is strategy in action. Napoleon did not enjoy a significantly unique insight into the character of contemporary warfare, let alone the eternal nature of war. Rather was his typical trademark an extraordinary practical ability to realize his intention and plans "in the field," adequately, in the face of enemies with independent wills and friction in all its many forms, predictable and other, the known as well as the "unknown unknowns."[26] Robert E. Lee needed corps and division commanders who both enjoyed some "strategic sense," but also who could fight their commands successfully in battle through the competent exercise of real- and near-real-time leadership.[27]

In the modern world, while it remains vital that strategy should be taught with close regard for its intellectual content, also, as just noted, there should always be recognition that ultimately it must be a practical, not a scholarly, pursuit. Education in strategy for potentially designated strategists is education with attitude. When strategic ideas are debated in a university seminar room to civilians, the students' strengths and weaknesses of character are not likely to have much bearing upon their subject. After all, they will not be required to turn in a strategic performance in a live military or political-military context. Philosophers, even superb ones, are encouraged to harbor doubt. They may weave an unsteady path in brilliant opinions from erudite book to erudite book. One can be something of a military philosopher and conduct oneself likewise, possibly as a slave to the latest popular epiphany. But a general as practicing strategist does not seek truth unadorned, rather he requires a contextually good enough truth for him to perform successfully the task at hand. In professional military strategic education, the quality of both strategy and strategist are vital. The former is irrelevant if the latter is unable to get it done, almost no matter how well he understands the structure of the challenge.

At this juncture we will both step back from consideration of the fundamentals of strategy and its performance by people who we can call strategists, and look forward to the strategic and other contexts of 21st century conflicts for which their skills will be needed.

21st Century Conflict.

If a person can think strategically, no matter whether this facility is acquired largely from nature or from nurture, he can do so about anything. The skill is indifferent to subject. That said, the strategist with talent, if not genius, needs the contextual specifics for flexibly adaptive application of strategy's general theory. To explain, the general theory of strategy was as relevant to the behavior of the American Expeditionary Force (AEF) of 1917-18, as it is to the American forces fighting in Afghanistan today. But the contextual differences between the two cases are so enormous that it is easy to see why Clausewitz insisted upon only an educational role for theory, and not an historically prescriptive one.[28] A benign synergism from the effects of native wit and life experience may suffice to yield strategic competence, but we, and every other defense community, major and minor, are prudent in assuming that natural talent, though possibly not genius, is likely to be augmented by some formal education in the essentials of strategy. These basics can be accessed and possibly comprehended from the written texts that by wide agreement comprise the classical canon of (general) strategic theory. One can argue over the marginal entries to the canonical literature, but by and large there is all but universal, nonculturally specific, consensus on the most authoritative works.[29] Obviously, this is good news for the educator. Rather less good news is the challenge to know what to teach aspiring strategists about their particular temporal domain of strategic history and its relevant contexts. We may nearly all agree on most of the elements that constitute strategy's general theory, and we can agree also broadly on how those elements function, or should function, interdependently. But, agreement diminishes rapidly once we can leave the relatively settled and secure zone of eternal and universal theory and venture upon the perilous terrain of actual strategies for today and tomorrow. It is necessary never to forget that no matter how robust and historically bullet-proof is our general theory, such wisdom can only be useful if it is adopted and adapted for all too particular historical needs in operational strategies-as-plans. For a vitally associated point, just as the elegant and dazzling insights of general theory do not themselves, and should not be expected to, deliver practical strategic value, for that one needs translation into specific strategies, so the strategist educated in theory has to perform strategically in practice.[30] But what kind of strategic practice can be anticipated today?

Although it is commonplace to postulate a spectrum of conflict, there is probably more value in conceiving of future conflict by means of a (or several) Venn diagram(s). Rather than approaching warfare conceptually along a spectrum ranging from most irregular to most regular, one should favor a model that is nonlinear and which does not even imply a prospective reality to option purity. Overlap is a quality that requires respect. This argument reads like an endorsement for the concept of "hybrid" wars.[31] In a sense that is so, but this theorist is not enthusiastic about adjectival qualifiers to the terms war, warfare, and strategy. The historical record shows incontestably that nearly all wars have been more or less "hybrid." It is neither historically accurate, nor especially useful, to suggest to the unwary that there is a distinctive species of conflict now known as "hybrid." Nonetheless, the adjective has some existential merit in that it points to such an important characteristic of wars and warfare that one might choose to regard hybridity as being in the very nature of war. Strategists today have to grasp the holism of their subject, and that subject must accommodate conflict, competition, rivalry, dueling, war, warfare, and strategy itself. The character of every conflict is to a degree distinctive. Moreover, nearly all conflicts have so-called regular and irregular features. And those features were present at one and the same time, often in the same conflict spaces. Conflict in the 21st century primarily most likely will be neither regular nor irregular, but in some measure nearly always significantly mixed or "hybrid" in character. Similarly, to cite another large but somewhat opaque descriptor, conflict will be asymmetrical. Only rarely are belligerents and their preferred styles in warfare very closely matched.

Given that there is no way of predicting exactly which conflicts will engage the professional skills of America's strategists in the future, there is no prudent alternative other than to prepare them for the full range of competitive possibilities in peace and especially in war. It is an elementary challenge to claim persuasively that future conflicts will be largely irregular in character. Ergo, American strategic education needs to privilege the skill set most suitable for effectiveness in irregular warfare. For some good reasons, the distinctive competencies for counterinsurgency (COIN) and counterterrorism (CT) are fashionable. But the story of today ought to be seen not as a shift away from focus on a regular style of warfare. Instead, the narrative ought to be one of a belated recovery of lost skills, in the context of ever necessary other military capabilities. Because we believe that we understand the conflicts of the 2000s, with their highlighting of the phenomenon of the "accidental guerrilla," we need to be alert to the danger that our new found confidence will prove largely misplaced should we assume it to be authoritative for the conflicts of the years to come.[32] The no-name post-Cold War era endured barely for a decade, from December 1991 until September 2001. The first decade of the 21st century may both merit the label the (or an) Age of Terror, but historical perspective and moderate prudence suggest that this era also is likely to be brief. Terrorism will always be with us, but it always has been, more or less. It is not at all anachronistic to claim that interstate, indeed greater and great, power rivalries are distinctly alive and well today. The currencies of power in world politics continue to include the military instrument.

Although economic globalization is a significant reality, it is thoroughly unmatched by political, cultural-moral, and truly authoritative legal globalization. The latter domains continue to be critically state-, certainly nation-, dominated. For illustration, Russia's Gazprom has indeed gone global, but it has done so in ways, and for reasons, that have everything to do with Russian geopolitical interests.[33] Similarly, although the Chinese economy does globalization by most definitions, the process has been guided by an official determination that the country must be more powerful as well as more wealthy. The two do not march inalienably in lock-step. For example, although the European Union (EU) is wealthy by any standard, if unevenly so, its footprint as a player in the enduring game of power politics is quite disproportionately light.

The spectrum (or, alternatively, the Venn diagram) of 21st century conflict embraces the complete range of possibilities. Interstate conflict is a reality today, though a reality currently in the backseat of history to a prevalence of intrastate and transstate conflict. Contemporary strategic education cannot afford to neglect any character of conflict, no matter what current fashion predicts and anticipates.

Those who strive to educate in grand and military strategy can be confident that their mission will always be necessary. This is sad, but, again unarguably, true. Louis J. Halle explained why when he advised that "Thucydides, as he himself anticipated, wrote the history of the Napoleonic wars, World War I, World War II, and the Cold War."[34] The Greek historian's tersely compounded explanation of the primary motives in statecraft — "fear, honor, and interest" — are as valid for the 21st century as they were for the 5th century BCE (Before the Common Era, formerly known as BC or Before Christ). To amplify the point, other leading trinitarian explanations have a like enduring authority. There is Clausewitz's trinity of passion, chance, and reason, to which one could add Kautilya's specification of the sources of power: intellect, wealth and military strength, and psychology.[35] For the basic structure of a human history that has always been strategic, we have the familiar triadic formula of ends, ways, and means. Thucydides donates the necessary conceptual tools, which we have to augment with sufficient specific details to render them operational. He explains why there will continue to be conflict and war in this century, as in all previous ones, but his brilliant triptych cannot be employed to predict individual wars. Nonetheless, for the educator it is more than merely helpful to be able to explain so elegantly and persuasively the fundamental motives that will shape policy and strategy in the future.

To teach about 21st century conflict is a challenge greatly eased by the elemental distinction between continuity and discontinuity. We know for certain that in the future there will be conflicts, including wars, and again for certain, in general terms, we know why there will be conflicts and wars. But what we do not and cannot know is exactly which rivalries will become conflicts which will erupt into wars. There is both good and bad news in this story. The bad news is that rivalry, conflict, and war are assured future realities. The better news is that no particular political rivalry inexorably and unavoidably must transition into conflict and war.

Poverty in political and strategic education has been responsible for a great deal of naïve, and therefore necessarily incompetent, policymaking since the Union of Soviet Socialist Republics (USSR) filed definitively for reorganization in December 1991. Neither the appearance of geopolitical discontinuity in world history effected by the end of the Cold War, nor the acceleration of an economic and information technology (IT)-led process of globalization, has imposed any significant change upon the fundamental working of intercommunity relations (interstate and intrastate). But so much of the detail has altered that scholars, politicians, and other commentators who should know better, have spoken, and even behaved, as if the apparent geopolitical revolution of 1991 had altered the nature of competitive political life. Politics is about power; it always has been and always will be. And when power, which is a dynamic relative quantity, as well as a value, is contested among security communities, the possibility of organized violence, military force, is imprinted in the DNA of the context.

It is easy to overprivilege the sad continuity in human political conflict, with its often present possibility of violence, and as a consequence adopt unwisely a fatalistic attitude. That said, it is well to remember that just as the first charge on an army is that to be effective at its most distinctive core competency, which is combat, so strategists should not shrink from their professional duty to study the politically purposeful use of force. Because many lands, most of the time, do not suffer from the curse of Mars, it does not follow that it is cynical, anachronistic, or in any way inappropriate for students of strategy to worry constructively about possible, if not necessarily actual, challenges to national and international security. And we know that those challenges in the 21st century must embrace rather more variants of conflict and warfare, probably all of them somewhat "hybrid," than the first decade of the century has revealed.

History (which is to say, historians) does not tell us what to expect, but it does provide warnings that should be unmistakeable and which we ignore at our most acute peril. It is not only useful, it is literally vital, that we acknowledge the certainty of historical discontinuities, at least the appearance of such, in the future. The reason that this matters so vitally is because unless we register as facts the coming of some known, suspected, and genuinely unknown unknowns, it is not possible for us to conduct prudent defense planning. The (military) strategist in time of peace, at least in a time mercifully innocent of the conduct of warfare on a massive scale, will lack reliable feedback on his/her competitive performance. How good is the general who has yet to command in warfare? How fit for its purpose will be the U.S. military posture of, say, 2019 or 2029, given that much, perhaps most, of that political purpose may not be extant in detail more than a year or a month ahead of the time that calls for action? It is obvious wisdom, and has to be sound advice, to recommend safely that our strategists should conduct U.S. defense planning obedient to a rule of minimum regrets. The test for adequate strategic performance in peacetime must be adaptability and flexibility, not excluding suitability for unfashionable categories of future conflict and warfare.[36] Looking in our historical rear-view mirror, we can see that the United States was appallingly unprepared militarily for the opening phase of the three great wars of the 20th century.[37] Future political shock is guaranteed by the nature of human history, just as is a military strategic dimension to that history. There is no discretion in the matter. We will be hugely surprised, and we will have need of a military instrument fit enough for the political character of the conflictual context at issue.

No matter how hard one tries, there is no escaping the perspective of today when we strive to educate for tomorrow. What I have claimed, not merely suggested, is that although we cannot possibly teach the history of a 21st century that still has 90 years to run, in fact, we know a great deal about those years, both near and distant. Our general theory of statecraft and strategy yields more than just adequate assistance in the crucial task of knowing how to think about the future. The major problem is how to cope well enough with the certain and identified challenges of today and the immediate future, without allowing ourselves to be captured by the "presentist" fallacy of believing that tomorrow is visible in the events and apparent trends of 2009. Strategic education must in part be fueled by appreciation of the ever shifting detail of history, but it should never be led by, and certainly it ought not to be confined to, the study of current events or contemporary history, for a slightly more elevated term. Strategists "educated" almost entirely by today would be uneducated for tomorrow's "today." Indeed, such erroneous education would not be education at all.

How to Teach Strategy.

In his recent study of Anglo-American grand strategy and strategists in World War II, historian Andrew Roberts claims credibly that "[m]ore often the Britons and Americans would take up positions according to nationality, but sometimes alliances were formed across both professional *and* national lines; just as politicians had to master strategy, so the soldiers were forced to become political."[38] Each profession was obliged by the bridging nature of strategy to operate outside its high comfort zone. Politicians are typically on thin ice when they contribute to military strategy, while soldiers must overcome skill, ethical, and sometimes even legal, challenges, when they are required to offer advice, and more, on subjects that transcend the narrowly military. It is possible, and I believe it is necessary and beneficial, to distinguish in theory among politics, policy, and grand strategy/ national security strategy. But there is no doubt that in practice, quite frequently in history, the three concepts essentially are fused or collapsed each into the others inextricably. It should be needless to add that this reality can be a source of deep discomfort to some professional soldiers. One has to qualify the argument by referring only to "some" soldiers, because every generation of military professionals, everywhere, contains at least a few generals who have the talent and personality for politics. They just happen to have taken the military road relatively early in life. For reasons that do not need rehearsing here, in democratic polities of most varieties, as well as in democracies of a more "guided" and "administered" kind (Vladimir Putin's Russia describes itself as an "administered democracy"), soldiers are either required or are strongly recommended to abstain from political activity. This is not to deny that the concept of the political is fit for inconclusive disputation.

The relevance of these remarks pertains, with some discomfort, to the realities of the practice of strategy in the zone where politics and the military instrument meet, which is to say on or very close to the metaphorical "strategy bridge." In an idealized world, for good or ill, and probably mainly for the latter, the (typically) civilian policymaker says "go get them" — this clearly is a lawful command from the distinctive world of policy — and the top soldier of the polity salutes, says "yes, sir!" and proceeds, unimpeded subsequently by political harassment, to exercise his professional skill as a soldier. The army is mobilized, and military strategy is determined according to the ways best suited to achieve the military goals that would translate as the military victory that policy demands. Of course, this simple narrative is a nonsense, and it always has been. In practice, policy is produced by politics, and because politics is a continuous process, so policy will shift. Moreover, all military strategy is grand strategy, though the latter is greater than the former, and the military professionals cannot responsibly simply take orders to fight from the realm of policy. The policy choices that they need to translate into military goals need to be calibrated with consideration of military ways and means. This is but the tip of the iceberg of the contextual interdependencies that staple the military professional as strategist to distinctly nonmilitary factors for consideration. How can strategy be taught, given its complexities and the real-world domination of contingency? Strategic surprise is a subject that this theorist addressed some years ago in a monograph for the Strategic Studies Institute.[39]

Paradoxically, and even ironically, the principal challenge to the would-be strategic educator is far easier than it appears. With Clausewitz as our leading mentor, we have to recognize that although it is necessary for senior generals to have a good base of knowledge on many subjects, there is no requirement for them to be a walking, or helicoptered, encyclopedia, a true polymath. The United States does not need its generals to know everything; rather does it need them to know what they have to know and, more important still, it needs them to know how to find out what they should know. Since the 1800s, the military profession in most countries has invented and developed modern staff systems so that the commanding general, even if he happens to be a genius, does not need to know everything himself. Also, given the size and complex articulation of armies, it has long been impossible even for genius to do almost everything himself.[40] But, beyond the acquisition of information it is necessary that the general, and general-to-be, should gain knowledge. However, knowledge itself, let alone information, is of no value to command performance in pursuit of the strategic effect that is the purpose of strategy. The human being in the uniform has to be able to extract understanding from his knowledge, and he needs the ability to use that understanding for the effective exercise of goal-focused command.

To answer the question "How should strategy be taught?" it is necessary first to be both clear and realistic about the exercise of the strategic function. Too often, institutions of higher military education do not ask themselves just what, or who, it is that they are attempting to teach. Should such a college seek to teach the body of professional lore that passes muster as "strategy," meaning the classics and near classics of strategic theory? Or do they really have in mind the education of people who might be promotable to be designated, formally or less so, as "strategists." As much to the point and to be blunt, should one concentrate on teaching the subject of strategy, or the whole person of the strategist? All of strategic history, not least as it is interpreted in the pages of *On War*, tries to tell us that we should teach the people who are educable those things in which they can be instructed, while recognizing and to a degree encouraging the creativity that an insightful intelligence will allow and generate. Creative genius, alas, is not the only kind of genius of which a country stands in need. In addition, it requires of its creative strategist(s) the ability to turn brilliant insights into effective command performance. In other words, it is not sufficient to educate strategists who know what should be done, or at least what might with great boldness be attempted. Also, there is an absolute requirement for a few, fortunately probably only a very few, strategists who are people of action as well as creative thought. Such persons have to be good enough, though not distinguished, strategic thinkers, strategically minded planners, commanders, and leaders. Mastery of the strategic classics is necessary, but can never be enough. There is always need for the person who not only understands the vital concept of the "culminating point of victory," but also who is likely to be able to identify it in real time and not when it is much too late (e.g., not when one's troops reach the Volga or approach the Yalu).[41]

Without wishing to understate the awesome challenges of the strategist's role in the no man's land where politics/policy and military power meet—on that strategy bridge, yet again—neither should we fail to recognize the functional strategic education by everyday experience at lower levels of behavior. Regarded as it should be, as a function, intimately interconnecting the trinity of ends, ways, and means, it is indisputable that planning and command execution at every level of military life, and most civilian ones also, is in a basic functional sense "strategic." Platoon and company leaders in combat trouble have to resolve life and death conundrums that are composed structurally of ends, ways, and means. It ought to follow from this almost banal empirically universal fact, that education by practice in strategy is rather more extensive than commonly is appreciated. But for the killer challenge to what might be thought to be a very widespread functional strategic competence, the major difficulty for the strategist is currency conversion across categories of behavior. Yes, the tactician has to manage coherently his tactical ends, ways, and means, but there can be great difficulty converting the tactical advantage of a multitude of military engagements into a significant operational level gain. While the challenge to the overall military strategist, of course, has to be the necessity to employ operational success for advantage in the course of the war as a whole. As if that were not trouble enough, the superior military strategist is charged with so conducting his military orchestra of operational successes and failures, that his polity's political ambitions are advanced, if not necessarily secured. A point is reached beyond which the battlefield will have contributed all that it is able, and the game of politics is played wholly by politicians, albeit by politicians who are likely to need the coercive value of some military menace slightly off-stage.

It is necessary to admit that although much of high importance about strategy can and should be taught, as we develop in the next section, also there is much that cannot be learnt by anything other than firsthand experience. Although there is a great deal to be said in favor of learning about strategy from the mistakes of others, it has to be admitted that nothing can compete in effectiveness with a truly personal impact. Dr. Samuel Johnson (especially as rephrased felicitously by John Gaddis, as quoted here) offered this relevant thought: "danger is a school for strategy."[42] The doctor's wise words, modernized by Gaddis, present a significant thought that has much merit. But it must be noted as a potent caveat that challenge need not stimulate an effective response, intellectual, moral, or physical. Learning by doing is more likely to educate the educable strategist better than is education by observation. Personal experience of the strategic function at the levels of higher military command has no close substitutes in the form of educational approaches. There is probably some value to the military historical tourism known generically as the staff ride.[43] And certainly there is merit in role playing games of several kinds. But for the military profession, as for all others, by far the best education is taught by the successes and especially the failures of personal practice.

The military profession frequently does its best to educate for higher command by manufacturing the virtual experience of such command in a variety of educational (and testing) exercises. A mixture of rides, simulations, historical and hypothetical future case studies, seminar debates, field exercises with troops, and deep and wide personal reading, all contribute to the effort to educate for the practice of strategy.[44] There are limitations as well as strengths inherent in every one of the components of the strategic educational process just cited. However, to say this is not to say anything especially profound or helpful. The methods noted here are dwarfed in their relative significance for the education of strategists by these four dominant factors: nature (biology), personality, experience, and opportunity. To these imperial four, we must add the difficult yet vital element of a wise military promotion and command selection system. It is simply a fact that politics, broadly defined, is not always a constructive element in the drive for military effectiveness. Although failure is widely recognized to be a teacher superior to success, military establishments are prone to punish failure. The paradox can be that although a major general learns his trade in good part by his errors as a divisional commander, that failure is judged by the command selection process not as valuable learning experience, but rather as sufficient proof of unfitness for corps command. Of course, this is not to suggest eccentrically that soldiers should be rewarded for failure. Obviously, some cases of failure in command will reflect all too accurately an unfitness for the level of responsibility attained. Every organization, including military ones, both overpromotes people who shone in lesser jobs, and terminates or effectively freezes the careers of people who are not permitted much slack in assessment of their current performance. It is neither useful nor fair to hold military organizations to a standard of perfection. Mistakes will always be made. Only in Lake Woebegone are all students above average.

The problem of education for strategists for the military profession is two-fold. First, the profession in a particular country can find itself for many years quite bereft of true experience in the exercise of its most core competency, fighting. Second, the strategic function is almost incomparably more important for professional soldiers than it is for other walks of life, because national security and human survival are at stake. When generals make mistakes, casualties ensue additional to those that are expected statistically (normal for the event). Furthermore, the whole community is apt to be placed in peril of several varieties as a consequence of poor military strategic performance. Early in the 20th century, it was a cynical French commonplace to quip that "it takes 20,000 casualties to train a major-general." Exaggeration though that may have been, it did make a necessary point that our current age likes to forget. It is a regrettable but unavoidable truth of military strategy that its primary instrument is the fighting power of its soldiers (however equipped for combat in whatever geographical environment). Western society with its decent liberal values teaches its citizens that every human life is an end in itself. But for the military strategist, his soldiers are individual pieces of his instrument, they cannot be valued principally as human beings whose safety is their commander's dominant concern. If the avoidance of casualties is "job one," the military instrument will be ineffective at best and prone to disaster at worst. Happily, there is no real conflict between a commander's "duty of care" for his men, and his duty to perform his command function. The latter is conducted in a manner that reflects the former. Indeed, if the command performance by a practicing strategist obviously expresses a wholly uncaring instrumental disregard for his individual soldiers, he will soon discover that their combat performance reflects their sense of betrayal.

Plainly, strategic education should strive to be as realistic as proves feasible. Fortunately for society but unfortunately for strategic education, on-the-job education for strategy in truly higher military command under wartime conditions tends to be relatively rare. On the one hand, most of the world's armed forces, most of the time, are not at war. On the other hand, even when a military establishment is at war, the number of higher command positions will always be very few. What this means is that history provides few opportunities for the people who are charged with the practice of military strategy to have a significant quality of directly relevant experience. Paradoxically, the more effective a military force is as a peacekeeping deterrent, the less likely it is to be effective on *der Tag* for action against specific enemies in the actual battlespace. Practice rarely makes perfect, but militaries that do not have to fight are unlikely to be good, let alone excellent, at first when the key is turned for war. Peace loving democracies almost invariably lose the "first fight" for this reason. To resort to a familiar adventurous analogy, it is probable that it is at least as difficult to excel as a brain surgeon as it is to succeed as a military strategist at the highest level. But whereas the brain surgeon hones his skills throughout his career, the military strategist does not.[45] There is always the distinctive problem of the enemy. The strategist needs to learn how to win in a rivalry, a competition, a "duel on a larger scale."[46] Few brains (subjects, victims) purposefully devise a cunning plan to thwart the surgeon's plan and his performance with the knife.

We must conclude this part of the discussion by advising, on the one hand, that it is obviously true to maintain that superior education for strategy can only be through its practice. On the other hand, military institutions are able to provide at least some educational assistance to those few people whom nature and personality have equipped to be candidates for the responsibilities of strategy. But, what should be taught as strategic education, and why? It is to these educationally operational topics that this monograph now turns.

What to Teach?

Above all else, the strategist has need of an educated capacity for strategic judgment. At its higher levels, which is to say, where operations must be conceived, planned, and executed for the purpose of shaping the whole military course of a war and where military goals need to be chosen for their anticipated political consequences, the strategist has to fly largely by intuition and guesswork. Certainly, what can be calculated should be calculated, but even supposedly authoritative metrics often are nothing of the sort. The strategist and his staff must calculate logistic needs and logistic availability, but the desperation of necessity can make some, not all, mockery of standard numbers. Casualty rates, their impact upon unit cohesion and morale, and the resulting reduction in combat effectiveness, can all be modeled and counted, but frequently they are counted incorrectly. The reason for this is that several or more factors contribute to human behavior, and readily PowerPointable elementary truths have a long history in the frustration of theory. For example, although combat power is enabled vitally by material factors, the immaterial, or moral elements as an earlier generation expressed it, are more important. Better men (on the day) with worse weapons will usually beat worse men with better weapons. Skill and determination matter more than the latest technology. There are, of course, practical contextually specific limits to this mighty truth. The prudent strategist will hope and strive to command both better men and better weapons.

Whether or not a person entrusted with strategic duties will prove capable of discharging them adequately is always, as noted already, determined by a mixture of nature, educated nurture, experience, and opportunity. American history no doubt has been well stocked with soldiers who would, perhaps could, have been distinguished strategists, had only their country called them to that duty. It might be an instructive exercise to review the fairly bloody history of the United States and pose the question, "when, and for how long, did the country need the services of outstanding strategists?" It is a truth of strategic history that even talented strategists can only demonstrate such proficiency as circumstances permit. Some enemies pose greater challenges than others. Some wartime contexts impose greater constraints on strategic talent than others. Political competence in the White House should provide a wartime playing field for America's military strategists that is distinctly uphill for the country's foes. Strategy is strategy, but most enemies of a power as well resourced as the United States should be defeatable for reasons that need not include American strategic brilliance. Strategic competence, shading into excellence, not brilliance, is the practicable goal that should be sought in the performance of the country's strategists.

For the limited purpose of this discussion, I am obliged to assume that the armed forces are competent in selecting for formal education in strategy those men and women who are strategically educable. In addition to their tactical grasp of "soldiering" in current conditions, which is to say their competent understanding of the "grammar of war" today,[47] I shall assume also that those selected for the higher education at issue here are competent and more in the management, command, and leadership of people. Somewhat more hesitantly, I need to assume that, in addition, the aspiring strategists have the physical and mental robustness and personalities that do not disable them from effective sustained command performance. The reason why it is necessary to proffer these terms of reference is because I need to identify just what a formal education in strategy might achieve, and what must be beyond its reach. Academic education cannot provide absent cognitive capacity, real-world experience of strategizing with awesome responsibilities, or a personality that commands respect, trust, and sometimes even affection. We professors should recognize our limitations.

Readers are advised that highly though I rank the value of some academic education in strategy, I am not misled into the self-flattering belief that we academics can teach strategy to officially designated strategists so well that success should be theirs. War and warfare are too complex to be reducible to an elementary contest between friendly and enemy skills in strategy. Having granted this caveat, I will proceed to specify what can and should be taught in an academic setting, albeit a setting enlivened with such exposure to the real world of relevant mud and blood as inspired teaching methods can offer usefully. The argument here is organized within the framework of seven major points.

First, students must be encouraged to think strategically.[48] They need to learn to focus upon actions as enablers of the consequences they seek. They have to reason as it were instrumentally, to try to anticipate second-and–beyond order effects. The tactician "does" for higher — broader, deeper, even distant — ends. Where military strategy as a coherent component of grand strategy meets the political world of policy, strategists have to be able to guess (calculate, intuit?), what particular intended operational-level military achievements bring to the big game of the whole military course of the war. And also, working with officials on the policy bank of the strategy bridge, the military strategist must identify the military objectives that should serve the political goals set by policy as the purpose of the enterprise. In Clausewitz's immortal words, "[t]he political object — the original motive for the war — will thus determine both the military objective to be reached and the amount of effort it requires."[49] This simple formula is as logically compelling as it is fearsomely difficult to apply in practice. In many wars, if not most, it will be far from self-evident, let alone calculable, how military achievements would translate into sufficient political success. Moreover, as we shall emphasize, it is necessary for would-be strategists to be educated for a competitive context, one which contains an enemy, or enemies, with an independent will(s).

To think strategically is to reason ends-ways-means. Too often in practice, relations among the three components in the triptych of the strategy function are not connected as just specified. Fashionable ways can drive means and the policy to legitimize them. Or, favored means may shape ways which drive ends — for truly multiple pathologies.[50] Suffice it to say that although the educated strategist will appreciate the potential for some disarrangement of the three elements, he will not be confused about the necessity for there to be tolerably coherent relations among them. Those ill-educated in strategy are liable to confuse ends, ways, and means, or at least are likely to be misled into strategic error by permitting the pressing demands of the instrument of war to dominate its purpose.

For an especially blatant historical example of a perilous misuse of concepts, consider the difficulty of thinking strategically about so-called Strategic Forces. When a military instrument itself is collapsed into its consequences what tends to be the result is what has been called the "tacticization of strategy."[51] In the 1960s, the irony was widely noted that U.S. tactical airpower functioned allegedly strategically against the territory of North Vietnam, while the quintessentially supposedly strategic B-52s of the Strategic Air Command performed tactical "Arc Light" strikes in the south. The trouble with such linguistic conceptual misuse and abuse is that it encourages dysfunctional thinking, planning, and behavior. When the United States has forces that it titles "strategic," what does it mean for forces that lack that once fashionable and prized label? Is the U.S. Army inherently nonstrategic? How can any among the elements that comprise the U.S. armed forces be other than strategic in the consequences of their threat or use? The student who is able to think strategically about landpower is enabled thereby to think strategically about any form of military power. An education in strategy must be founded upon a rock solid grasp of the intimate desirable relations among ends, ways, and means, and he should be able to detect undue slighting of one component in favor of the others. Policy without matching ways and means is mere vanity, while absent policy, actions by ways with available means has to be pointless.

Second, some formal education in strategic theory is desirable for all aspiring strategists. Nonetheless, there will usually be someone who has no need of book learning on strategy; a person who knows what Clausewitz should have written, even if he did not quite write it—insofar as one can tell across language, culture, and time. However, exposure to the classics typically does no harm, even to those whose natural endowments and learning from long experience might render such an exercise redundant. Few among history's greater strategists might not have improved their performances had they been better educated. It is a safe assumption that everyone whose future duties could be intelligently tagged as strategic should benefit from the education achieved by others. The others in this case are by widespread assent the most perceptive among those who have ever sought to understand and explain war and warfare. Because statecraft and war have not changed their natures over the millennia, the very few true classics of strategy are works that by definition must speak meaningfully for our time, as they do for all others.[52] If we can assume, as we must, that the contemporary would-be strategist is tactically a master of his profession, and what he does not know he can readily find out, it is evident that his education in strategy need not be tied to any particular historical strategic context. In point of fact, it is probably desirable that his educators in strategy divert him from current and future topics of concern. Speaking on February 22, 1947, at Princeton University, Secretary

42

of State General George C. Marshall proffered the opinion that he doubted "whether a man can think with full wisdom and with deep convictions regarding certain of the basic international issues today who has not at least reviewed in his mind the period of the Peloponnesian War and the Fall of Athens."[53] Whether or not the general overstated his case, nonetheless, it was a powerful case worthy of overstatement. Since statecraft and war have changed only their character, but not their nature, over the centuries, it has to follow that a common general theory of strategy should apply to all historical examples of the phenomena. A prime source of the benefit of learning grand and military strategy from Pericles of Athens and King Archidamus of Sparta—courtesy of Thucydides—has to be the distance in detail from the student's military culture. To be educated in strategy via such instructive and bloody episodes as Athens' Sicilian Expedition of 415-413 BCE, or Napoleon's adventure in Russia in 1812, avoids the danger of military institutional or national parochialism and bias that is apt to intrude upon the contemplation of contemporary issues.

Third, although education in strategy must have as its backbone a general theory that is both timeless and universal in authority, strategy is a practical subject, and its executors must learn how to employ that theory for its current value. General theory advises the practicing strategist about the structure and working of his professional function. But, following Clausewitz closely, I must insist that such education can only teach the strategist how to approach his duties as strategist, it cannot instruct or train in the contemporary content, the officer himself must provide for the classic ideas to fit the specific context.[54] Possible illustrative examples abound. Center(s) of gravity (COG) is a powerful notion that militaries are apt to find irresistible, and for some good reasons.[55] But rarely is this contestable idea entirely beyond dispute as to its nature, character, precise location(s), and relevance to the strategic challenge of the day. Only contemporary assessment of context can determine the identity of the most relevant COG. And only contextual analysis is able to reveal whether it is advisable, or even feasible, to menace the enemy's COG.

The strategic educator is obliged most strictly to distinguish strategic general theory (singular), from the concrete historical specifics that have to shape and drive plans and strategies (plural) for the actual practice of strategy. Considered in the abstract by categories, there is nothing in 21st century statecraft and warfare that did not exist in the 5th century BCE. The relative significance of every dimension to strategy will alter from period to period, war to war, and even month to month in the same war. For example, the commanders of an army proud of its maneuverist dexterity may discover that geography and logistics can trump operational military skill. The German Army in Russia (*Ostheer*) in 1941 tried successfully to educate the future soldiers of all nations in the realities of supply and movement as limitations to operational ambition.

The educator in strategic theory is neither a philosopher in the search of truth for its own sake, nor is he promoting ideas in contradistinction to action. Strategic theory and purposeful strategic practice are indissolubly connected. The military planner is, *ipso facto*, a theorist. A plan is a theory specifying how a particular goal might be secured, *ceteris paribus*. Until the course of future events unfolds, the chief planner and the commander, who may be one and the same person, are deciding and acting only on the basis of a theory of success. Because even classic theorists of strategy have been known to weave in their literary narratives among what today we know as policy, strategy, operations, and tactics, strategic education has to be alert to the ever present necessity to distinguish between the continuities and the discontinuities in strategic history. Great abstract ideas—such as war's trinitarian nature, friction, COG, and many others—always need translation in detail for today, as well as proper comprehension, of course. It follows that although strategic debaters can hardly avoid argument by purported historical analogy, so critical to useful applicability is the detail of context that alleged evidence by illustration must be virus-checked for lethally inappropriate anachronism.

Fourth, wherever strategic education may fall short, prominent among the more harmful of its potential areas of neglect would be a failure to emphasize the pervasive importance of the enemy. Underappreciation of the inherently competitive nature of a strategic context probably has been the most damaging source of poor to catastrophic historical strategic performance. The leading source for the paradox and irony that Edward N. Luttwak so brilliantly exposes as being central to the very nature of strategy is the presence of an independent, indeed interdependent, player on the field—the enemy.[56] Luttwak draws suitable attention to the necessity of understanding the enemy; a good practice that has been valid since earliest times. Sun-tzu, Thucydides, and Clausewitz, were all eloquent in their several ways on the subject of the importance of trying to know the enemy. It is easily understandable, though it is not readily forgivable, for military texts to have little to say about the competitive nature of war, warfare (and statecraft). With his central focus on paradox in strategy, Luttwak is unique among the classic theorists of strategy in treating the subject of war as a duel with the full seriousness that it merits. Indeed, if anything, his analysis may risk overstatement. Even an excellent idea, a truly penetrating insight, can be overworked.

As usual in all matters strategic, good advice tends to conceal real danger. It is necessary for soldiers to be bold, but not reckless. It is essential to respect the enemy, but not to stand in awe of him. In Korea in 1950, General Douglas MacArthur was bold at Inchon, but reckless in his drive to the Yalu. In the Western desert of North Africa in 1941-42, a succession of British generals and their troops came not merely to respect German General Erwin Rommel, rather they expected to be beaten by him. A classic wholly American example of this peril was the ill-effect on the morale of the Union's Army of the Potomac and its leaders of Robert E. Lee's well-merited reputation as a general who won his battles.[57] Confederate soldiers in the Army of Northern Virginia expected to win, and — prior to Gettysburg — their opponents anticipated defeat.

For the strategic educator, it is a challenge to know where general wisdom on warfare ends and local contextual variation begins. While there should be no argument over the significance of an *other* whose locally encultured mind is the object of our military (*inter alia*) effort, there is major scope for dispute over what should be regarded simply as universal best practice in the military context. To illustrate for clarity, would we anticipate Vietnamese irregular fighters waging their warfare in a notably Oriental, even Vietnamese-Oriental manner? Or, rather, in the same way any intelligent and well-motivated belligerent would behave in a similar context and situation?[58] Today's strategic educators need to beware lest inadvertently they miseducate, even if for excellent, though in context harmful, reasons. We know that every war is different, but how different is that? The classic texts on COIN can and must be taught for their enduring wisdom. But, failure to adapt Galula, Thompson, and now Kilcullen, to new contexts, most especially to new enemies, must fuel the prospects for strategic failure in the future.[59] Directly put, today's field-grade officers may be educated by their own command experience, an experience reinforced by new teaching in war colleges, to misunderstand the unforeseeable historical strategic challenges of COIN in the 2010s and beyond. War can move on more rapidly than fashion in the content of military education.

Fifth, as a separate item it is necessary for this monograph to highlight the significance of a skeptical, though not cynical, mindset as a strategic asset. This can be difficult to achieve, because although the experience of a lively military career should provide ample fuel for skepticism on the part of the successful soldier, the personality requirements for effective command can neutralize a healthy skepticism. By this I mean to suggest that a successful general is most likely to be one who is, or certainly who appears to be, self-confident. Skepticism is a crowning virtue in a philosopher. But we do not want our soldiers to be philosophers. To take action in the face of war's systemic uncertainty, to take chances with many men's lives, and especially to adhere to a plan when evidence of its possible unsoundness begins to accumulate — all these features, and many more, require the strategist-commander to be resolute, determined, and occasionally to turn a blind eye to orders from the fainter-hearted. All of that granted, still it is necessary for this monograph to register a vote for skepticism as a vital component in strategic education. The on-going, ever-renewed, American defense debate, in common with the debates in other defense communities, is prone to overpersuasion by apparent novelty in strategic ideas and methods. One must say "apparent," because generically there are no new ideas and methods in strategy and warfare. The classical canon of strategic texts contains, and repeats, them all. However, the U.S. defense community, with its multitude of stakeholder interests, its genuinely global challenges, and its awesome array of conceptual, organizational, technical, tactical, logistic, and social, issues—to specify only some of the categories—positively invites the marketing of novelty. Of course, just because the latest new idea lurks underappreciated in the pages of Sun-tzu, this does not mean that an old idea is not new to a strategically poorly educated audience that is vulnerable to seduction by a slick PowerPoint presentation. The strategist should be a creative thinker. But as Antulio Echevarria argues, "critical thinking is far more important to achieving a successful transformation than is creative imaginative thinking."[60] One could add that the better critical strategist might even dare to question whether transformation is desirable.

The argument here amounts simply to *caveat emptor*. What goes around, comes around. Bad ideas are certain to return in the next-but-one (or two, three, or four) strategic debate. An education in strategy worthy of the name helps significantly to inoculate aspiring strategists against hasty capture by ideas that have a less than glittering historical record, no matter how distant that record may be. It is not to be doubted, however, that a poor idea in one historical context can be a good idea in another. For an obvious example, it would be absurd to purport to promulgate some general wisdom about the proper relationship between ground power and air power, regardless of political, geographical, and technological, contexts.[61] The value of air power varies with terrain, weather, technology, and military-strategic circumstances. This fifth point is intended to reinforce the most central argument of this work; the claim that the overriding mission of an education in strategy has to be the enhancement of the strategist's ability to exercise judgment. For this essential function, he requires knowledge, especially historical understanding, of what succeeded and failed in which circumstances in the past, and why. Because it is a pragmatic project, strategic competence, let alone excellence, is a matter not only of recognizing ideas and methods that have high promise. Competence is at least as much a matter of being able to judge which ideas and methods appear to be fit enough for the purposes of the day.

For a closing word on skepticism, though one that strays unmistakeably into outright cynicism, I quote these words from the perceptive British novelist of military follies, Derek Robinson:

> Your problem is you're personally offended when you discover a cock-up. Believe me, there's *always* a cock-up. It's in the nature of war. Whoever said truth is the first casualty arrived late on the scene. The first casualty of war is the plan. . . . The first plan always fails. Usually the second plan does, often the third too. Then, with a bit of luck, the next plan works, and we win. That's my experience.[62]

Sixth, the advisability of an active capacity for skepticism needs to be balanced by a confidence that it is possible for the strategist and his strategy to function well enough for its task. To venture into dangerously complex terrain, I shall hazard the thought that the same skepticism that can be destructive of recognition of merit and of resolution, also serves in a vital critical role. Ideas, and ideas as plans, need to be interrogated for their strengths and weaknesses. Moreover, there are many situations in statecraft, war, and warfare, when the skeptical faculty illuminates a high danger of failure in every discernible option. In such a context, the strategist simply must benefit from the skepticism that alerts him to peril, and choose the course of action that in his judgment offers the best odds when danger and opportunity are compared and estimated. Strategic education has to inform the student about the argument advanced by some scholars, soldiers, and novelists, to the effect that strategy is impossible; allegedly it is an illusion.[63] That argument has some superficial plausibility, but it collapses definitively under the empirical weight of historical evidence. Strategy can be done and has been done, notwithstanding the myriad of impediments to its performance. An education in strategy most emphatically is not a foolish education in the impossible. Astrology is an example of nonsense, strategy is not.

Seventh, a strategic education should include an education in what today we know as the liberal arts. More broadly still, there seems to this strategic theorist to be some, though only some, significant correlations historically between educationally well-rounded people and outstanding performance in the higher realms of strategy. A narrow military competence can suffice, but there are good reasons why such must place the soldier under a heavy burden of inadequacy. To be specific, the strategist has no choice but to communicate with the political world, the realm whither policy guidance flows. Ideally, and notwithstanding the civil-military distinction that was so excellently overstated by Samuel P. Huntington, the very senior soldier should be able to explain the actual and prospective military story to professional politicians and civilian officials in a way that they can comprehend.[64] The soldier-strategist owes it to his army and country to explain the military context so that policy is shaped realistically. Many senior soldiers have had personalities adequate and more for the rise to the stratosphere of their profession, only to find that they could not be effective in communicating outside the military family. When this occurs, there is a danger that politicians will hire and fire military chiefs until they locate the men that seem to be suitably empathetic, or at least with whom some genuine dialog is possible. Even with good will on both sides, which is to say with a sincere intention to collaborate constructively, the strategic function which must be shared by soldier-strategists and politician-strategists is extremely difficult to perform well enough. A liberally educated soldier is more likely to be able to reach a civilian audience than is one whose enculturation has been limited to the necessities of his military duties. To be able to offer prudent military advice, senior soldiers have need of some political and social-cultural, as well as strategic, sense. It should go without saying, but I will say it anyway, that an educated strategist is a person who both possesses, and on occasion consults and is known to consult, a moral compass.

Conclusion.

This monograph suggests a legion of ideas, claims, and arguments, that might so warrant the stamp of authorial self-approval as to be itemized as conclusions.

Rather than offer recommendations as such, I choose instead to be content to recommend seven points to the reader for his consideration.

1. True strategic genius is rare indeed. Fortunately, the country usually has need only of strategic talent. The latter can be improved by some formal education in strategy conducted by institutions charged with that purpose; the former most probably cannot be enhanced, though it might be tamed. If anything, there could be a danger that formal education might blunt a talent of genius that is gifted by nature and has been honed by the opportunities granted by experience. One has to acknowledge that there is a sense in which strategic genius is what genius does, and that involves creative insight, strategic *coup d'oeil*, that cannot significantly be the product of the classroom.

2. Happily, the country can survive and prosper even without unarguable, though almost inevitably eccentric, even roguish, strategic genius. Instead, it requires the services of strategists who are good enough, who are "fit for purpose" as the saying goes. Just how challenging that purpose will be must vary with the details of historical context. A well-constructed curriculum and a wise mix of educational methods, certainly is able to teach what can be taught in order to help educate those who are educable in strategy.

3. Because good, not necessarily excellent, strategic performance requires some qualities in people that are extraneous to strictly intellectual understanding, there are aspects of strategy that cannot be taught. That granted, still there is much that can and has to be taught, not least because nearly everyone who has a genuine instinct for the sound higher conduct of

war — and there are few of these — can benefit from a little help.

4. The help that formal strategic education offers includes the aid to reasoning that is on offer in the classical canon of writings by those authors that by effectively universal consent have thought most deeply and perceptively about the subject. The would-be strategists of today cannot help but benefit from reading (with understanding) Clausewitz, Sun-tzu, and Thucydides, for the most sacred of authorial icons in the strategic canon, even, sometimes especially, when they disagree with their arguments.

5. The strategist's responsibility is awesomely difficult in good part because it is so inclusive in its required domain. The strategist must strive to provide a purposeful coherence to the realm of policy and tactics. The key to strategic sense may sound so obvious as to be banal when it is made explicit, as here. The strategist needs to be able to exercise sound strategic judgment. By that I mean no more and no less than the ability to juggle, perhaps manage and guide, creatively and coherently the practice of the strategic function which comprises the pursuit of ends, by suitable ways, employing appropriate means. At its highest level, the strategist has to attempt to orchestrate military and other behavior for desired political consequences. This is an inherently enormous challenge in currency conversion from military coin to political coin. Some education in strategic history cannot train a person regarding best practice for his historically unique strategic problems. But that education assuredly can educate today's strategist as to the kinds of behaviors that succeeded and failed in particular categories of a given situation. Although there is no historical permanence in details, there is much permanence in

the nature of strategic contexts. This is why the classics of strategy continue to have far more than mere antiquarian value.

6. Unbloodied and unmuddied by military experience, civilian would-be educators in strategy are potentially highly vulnerable to the fallacy of overintellectual "strategism." By this I mean that they are persuaded that strategy and its performance is largely an intellectual matter. They are at least half-correct. Strategy does have a significant intellectual dimension. Moreover, even when strategic judgment may seem more instinctual than intellectual, it is probably the case that the superior instinct was at least sharpened, and its operation may have been triggered, by ideas from a strategic classic that lodged in the brain in deep reserve against the call of a mercifully rare necessity. Because strategy is a pragmatic subject, it must be approached and performed via a coherently constructive fusion of relevant theory and practice. Strategy implies both a theory, including theory-as-plan, and performance: It has to be done.

7. The final point is cautionary. Those who would educate in and for strategy are ever vulnerable to another sin of "strategism." This is the belief that the key to America's prospects for success in this and that venture is sound strategy. I am prone episodically to capture by this fallacy. It is well to remember that although poor or absent strategy is likely to sink any military enterprise, great or small, it is by no means alone in such important status. It should be obvious that faulty policy is apt to be more lethal than is weak strategy. Or, what if policy ends are well chosen while strategic ways seem suitable, but, alas, the military and other means are tactically incapable of the needed perform-

ance in the field and on the day? Plainly, performance of the strategic function depends upon both the political purpose and the actions of the military members of the national security team.

ENDNOTES

1. F. E. Adcock, *The Roman Art of War Under the Republic: Martin Classical Lectures, Vol. VIII*, Cambridge, MA: Harvard University Press, 1940, p. 124.

2. Andrew F. Krepinevich and Barry D. Watts, "Lost at the NSC," *The National Interest*, No. 99, January-February 2009, available from BNET Find Articles, p. 4; and John Collins, *Grand Strategy: Principles and Practices*, Annapolis, MD: Naval Institute, 1973, p. 235.

3. *Ibid.*, p. 7.

4. Consideration of military, if not strategic, genius should begin with Carl von Clausewitz, *On War*, Michael Howard and Peter Paret, trans., Princeton, NJ: Princeton University Press, 1976, Book One, Ch. 3. An outstanding discussion is Hew Strachan, *Clausewitz's On War: A Biography*, New York: Atlantic Monthly Press, 2007, pp. 94-96, 127-129. In his three great military biographies, Carlo D'Este probes in depth the phenomena of genius (Patton, Churchill) and talent (Eisenhower). See his studies: *A Genius for War: A Life of General George S. Patton*, London: Harper Collins, 1995; *Eisenhower: A Soldier's Life*, New York: Henry Holt, 2002; and *Warlord: A Life of Churchill at War, 1874-1945*, London, UK: Allen Lane, 2009.

5. Thucydides, *The Landmark Thucydides: A Comprehensive Guide to The Peloponnesian War*, Robert B. Strassler, ed., New York: The Free Press, 1996, p. 43.

6. I prefer Antulio Echevarria's translation of *wunderliche* as "wondrous," to its translation as "remarkable" in Howard and Paret's 1976 edition of *On War*, and even to its translation as "paradoxical" in their second edition (1989). See Echevarria,

Clausewitz and Contemporary War, Oxford, UK: Oxford University Press, 2007, pp. 70-71, 81, n. 40.

7. Clausewitz, p. 32.

8. Wayne P. Hughes, Jr., "The Strategy-Tactics Relationship," in Colin S. Gray and Roger W. Barnett, eds., *Seapower and Strategy*, Annapolis, MD: Naval Institute Press, 1989, p. 47.

9. For explanation additional to that provided here, see Colin S. Gray, *The Strategy Bridge: Theory for Practice*, Oxford, UK: Oxford University Press, forthcoming, Ch. 6.

10. *Ibid.*, Appendix C; and Hew Strachan, "The Lost Meaning of Strategy," *Survival*, Vol. 47, No. 3, Autumn 2005, pp. 33-54. The first use of the word strategy in its modern meaning, which is to say beyond generalship narrowly, occurred in 1777 in books in French and German. English language dictionaries prior to 1810 did not contain a "strategy" entry. Linguistically, if not quite actually, what we identify distinctly as policy and strategy effectively were fused.

11. Clausewitz, p. 177.

12. *Ibid.*, p. 75; and J. C. Wylie, *Military Strategy: A General Theory of Power Control*, Annapolis, MD: Naval Institute Press, 1989, p. 66.

13. I was assisted in reaching this conclusion by Antulio J. Echevarria II, "Dynamic Inter-Dimensionality: A Revolution in Military Theory," *Joint Force Quarterly*, No. 15, Spring 1997, p. 36. "[A]ll events in war have weight; even the least can have disproportionate effects. For example, the personality of a commander looms as large as the size and preparedness of an army."

14. Gabriel Marcella and Stephen D. Fought, "Teaching Strategy in the 21st Century," *Joint Force Quarterly*, No. 52, 1st Quarter 2009, p. 57. "Strategy exists and is developed at every level, it is developed with the purpose of connecting political purpose with means."

15. Robert Lyman, *The Generals: From Defeat to Victory, Leadership in Asia, 1941-45*, London, UK: Constable, 2008, pp. 341.

16. Clausewitz draws an important distinction between the political "logic" and what he terms the "grammar" of war (p. 406). I share strongly Echevarria's view of this key relationship. He writes: "Again, neither logic nor grammar is meaningful without the other. Yet the history of war shows that the two are at odds more often than not." *Clausewitz and Contemporary War*, p. 145.

17. NATO's air war against the former Yugoslavia/Serbia in 1999 is a classic example. Controversy over the strategic and political effect of the 78-day air campaign continues to the present time. See Benjamin S. Lambeth, *NATOs Air War for Kosovo: A Strategic and Operational Assessment*, Santa Monica, CA: RAND, 2001; Daniel R. Lake, "The Limits of Coercive Airpower: NATO's 'Victory' in Kosovo Revisited," *International Security*, Vol. 34, No. 1, Summer 2009, pp. 83-112.

18. Clausewitz, p. 77 (emphasis in the original).

19. See Michael I. Handel, *Masters of War: Classical Strategic Thought*, 3rd ed., London, UK: Frank Cass, 2001, Appendix E.

20. Gray, *Strategy Bridge,* Appendix B.

21. A conference statement quoted with permission in Colin S. Gray, "Britain's National Security: Compulsion and Discretion," *The RUSI Journal*, Vol. 153, No. 6, December 2008, p. 18, n.5.

22. Bernard Brodie, *War and Politics*, New York: Macmillan, 1973, p. 452.

23. For a more complete and detailed treatment of the strategist's roles, see my *The Strategy Bridge*, Ch. 6.

24. Edward N. Luttwak's book, *The Grand Strategy of the Roman Empire: From the First Century A.D. to the Third*, Baltimore, MD: Johns Hopkins University Press, 1976, makes boldly anachronistic use of some modern strategic concepts. A strong attack on Luttwak, particularly for his argument that the Romans

had a grand strategy, is contained in Benjamin Isaac, *The Limits of Empire: The Roman Army in the East*, Oxford, UK: Clarendon Press, 1990, Ch. 9. I am grateful to the historian, Jeremy Black, for his view on the effective merger of policy and grand strategy in the thought of the 18th century. Strategy (English), *strategie* (French and German) was not recognized linguistically as a function distinctive from statecraft or generalship prior to the late 18th century. Polities did not have permanent or even temporary schools and military staff charged with "strategic" duties. Policy and strategy, though logically separable, usually were all but collapsed one into the other. Most especially was this true for what today we call grand (English) or national (American) strategy. For a related matter, although it is commonplace for us in English to distinguish between politics and policy, the German word *Politik* with which Clausewitz has somewhat frustrated some of his English interpreters, is actually a benign confusion. It is helpful and empirically sound to fuse politics and policy, unusual though this would be for American strategic thinkers. On this matter, see David Kaiser, "Back to Clausewitz," *The Journal of Strategic Studies*, Vol. 32, No. 4, August 2009, p. 681.

25. Norman F. Dixon, *On the Psychology of Military Incompetence*, London, UK: Future Publications, 1979. Dixon's book delivers more than a little insight, but it is flawed by much unpersuasive military history, as well as by oversimple psychologizing. I recommend that readers of Dixon's minor classic augment their psychological education on command by consulting Robert Pois and Philip Langer, *Command Failure in War: Psychology and Leadership*, Bloomington: Indiana University Press, 2004.

26. See Nathan Frier, *Known Unknowns: Unconventional "Strategic Shocks" in Defense Strategy Development*, Carlisle, PA: Strategic Studies Institute, U.S. Army War College, November 2008.

27. Robert E. Lee's paucity of subordinates who were competent, let alone inspired, in major battlefield command positions, is well explained in Joseph T. Glatthaar, *General Lee's Army: From Victory to Collapse*, New York: The Free Press, 2008, Ch. 26.

28. An "objective" understanding of war, warfare, and strategy must always be overlaid by a "subjective" grasp of the character of the contexts of the day. The objective/subjective distinction is borrowed from Clausewitz. The former should be eternal and universal truths; the latter refers to the transitory character of dynamic conditions. Clausewitz, p. 85. Echevarria, *Clausewitz on Contemporary War*, Ch. 1, "A Search for Objective Knowledge," is thoughtful, rigorous, and useful—a rare trio.

29. See my *Strategy Bridge*.

30. Alvin H. Bernstein made the point pungently when he recounted this (almost certainly personal) anecdote: "A young infantryman, after informing a professor that his presentation on Thucydides was the best lecture he had ever heard on any subject, then added with a Cheshire cat grin, 'Unfortunately, it didn't teach me squat about how to take that hill'." "Thucydides and the Teaching of Strategy," *Joint Force Quarterly*, No. 14, Winter 1996-97, p. 126.

31. See Frank G. Hoffman, *Conflict in the 21st Century: The Rise of Hybrid Wars*, Arlington, VA: Potomac Institute for Policy Studies, December 2007; *idem*, "Hybrid Warfare and Challenges," *Joint Force Quarterly*, No. 52, 1st Quarter 2009, pp. 34-39.

32. David Kilcullen's significant study, *The Accidental Guerrilla: Fighting Small Wars in the Midst of a Big One*, London, UK: C. Hurst, 2009, warns against confusing local sources of grievance with far larger ones. The grandiose notion of a global war on terror is the kind of adversary inflation that is a gratuitous self-inflicted American conceptual wound. To fast rewind temporally, the great Cold War also was peopled amply with accidental guerrillas who were misidentified as members of a universal legion for godless communism/Soviet imperialism.

33. See the lively but well-supported argument in Michael Stuermer, *Putin and the Rise of Russia*, London, UK: Phoenix, 2008, Ch. 8.

34. Louis J. Halle, *The Elements of International Strategy*, Lanham, MD: University Press of America, 1984, p. 15.

35. Clausewitz, p. 89; Kautilya, *The Arthashastra*, L. N. Rangarajan, trans., New Delhi, India: Penguin Books (P), 1992, p. 559.

36. I address the challenge of peacetime defense planning in my article, "Coping with Uncertainty: Dilemmas of Defense Planning," *Comparative Strategy*, Vol. 24, No. 4, July-September 2008, pp. 324-331.

37. Historical perspective is to be found in Charles E. Heller and William A. Stofft, eds., *America's First Battles, 1776-1965*, Lawrence: University Press of Kansas, 1986. It is not a pretty story. America usually, though not invariably, wins the last battle, which matters more than the first one. Nonetheless, faith in eventual success is cold comfort for those who are trapped in a present awfully shaped by unpreparedness.

38. Andrew Roberts, *Masters and Commanders: How Roosevelt, Churchill, Marshall and Alanbrooke Won the War in the West*, London, UK: Allen Lane, 2009, p. 5 (emphasis in the original).

39. Colin S. Gray, *Transformation and Strategic Surprise*, Carlisle, PA: Strategic Studies Institute, U.S. Army War College, April 2005. This monograph, very lightly edited, is also published in Colin S. Gray, *National Security Dilemmas: Challenges and Opportunities*, Washington, DC: Potomac Books, 2009, Ch. 4.

40. Some relevant history is offered in David T. Zabecki, ed., *Chief of Staff: The Principal Officers Behind History's Great Commanders*, 2 vols., Annapolis, MD: Naval Institute Press, 2008.

41. Clausewitz, pp. 566-573.

42. John Lewis Gaddis, "What Is Grand Strategy?" Lecture delivered at the conference on "American Grand Strategy after War," sponsored by the Triangle Institute for Security Studies and the Duke University Program in American Grand Strategy, February 26, 2009, p. 2. It may be recalled that the highly opinionated but sometimes perceptive Dr. Samuel Johnson expressed the thought that "[w]hen a man knows he is to be hanged in a fortnight, it concentrates his mind wonderfully." Samuel Johnson, *QuotationsBook.com*, 2005.

43. See David Ian Hall, ed., "The Relevance and Role of Military History, Battlefield Tours and Staff Rides for Armed Forces in the 21st Century," *Defence Studies*, Vol. 5, No. 1, March 2005.

44. On strategic education, see Williamson Murray, "The Army's Advanced Strategic Art Program," *Parameters*, Vol. XXX, No. 4, Winter 2000-01, pp. 31-39; David Auerswald, Janet Breslin-Smith and Paula Thornhill, "Teaching Strategy Through Theory and Practice," *Defence Studies*, Vol. 4, No. 1, Spring 2004, pp. 1-17; Jeffrey D. McCausland, *Developing Strategic Leaders for the 21st Century*, Carlisle, PA: Strategic Studies Institute, U.S. Army War College, February 2008; Stephen D. Chiabotti, "A Deeper Shade of Blue: The School of Advanced Air and Space Studies," *Joint Force Quarterly*, No. 49, 2nd Quarter 2008, pp. 73-76; and Marcella and Fought, "Teaching Strategy in the 21st Century." For an earlier generation of effort, see Gene M. Lyons and Louis Morton, *Schools for Strategy: Education and Research in National Security Affairs*, New York: Frederick A. Praeger, 1965. I am grateful to Lyons and Morton for their title, which I have borrowed shamelessly for this monograph.

45. I am deeply indebted to Michael Howard for this analogy. In one of the finest, if not the finest, essays ever written on military history, he notes as follows:

> [H]is [the professional soldier as commander] profession is almost unique in that he may have to exercise it only once in a lifetime, if indeed that often. It is as if a surgeon had to practise throughout his life on dummies for one real operation; or a barrister [courtroom attorney] appeared only once or twice in court towards the close of his career; or a professional swimmer had to spend his life practising on dry land for an Olympic championship on which the fortunes of his entire nation depended.

The Causes of Wars and other Essays, London, UK: Counterpoint, 1983, p. 214. This justly famous essay ("The Uses and Abuses of Military History") was written in 1961 and reprinted in *Parameters*, March 1981.

46. Clausewitz, p. 75.

47. *Ibid.*, p. 605.

48. Carl. H. Builder, "Keeping the Strategic Flame," *Joint Force Quarterly*, No. 14, Winter 1996-97, pp. 76-84, is outstanding in purpose, though alas not in conceptual rigor.

49. Clausewitz, p. 81.

50. Michael Howard has observed wryly that "the complex problem of running an army at all is liable to occupy his [senior military professional] mind and skill so completely that it is very easy to forget what it is being run *for*." *The Causes of War*, p. 214 (emphasis in the original). A policy decision for war is always at some risk to capture by its instrument. Policy can assume a supporting role, with the needs of war apparently in the lead. Thus, ways and means would command ends.

51. Handel, *Masters of War*, Appendix E.

52. I appreciate that the text here asserts a doctrine of "historical permanence" with which some, perhaps many, professional historians are not entirely comfortable. We social scientist strategists are willing to be less in awe of apparently distinctive historical contextuality. This is attributable in part to different, even somewhat rival, professional skill biases. See the thoughtful essay that addresses this point, Eliot A. Cohen, "The Historical Mind and Military Strategy," *Orbis*, Vol. 49, No. 4, Fall 2005, pp. 575-588.

53. Quoted in Paul A. Rahe, "Thucydides as Educator," in Williamson Murray and Richard Hart Sinnreich, eds., *The Past as Prologue: The Importance of History to the Military Profession*, Cambridge, MA: Cambridge University Press, 2006, p. 99.

54. Clausewitz, pp. 141, 578.

55. *Ibid.*, pp. 595-600.

56. Luttwak, *Strategy; idem*, "Strategy," in John Whiteclay Chambers II, ed., *The Oxford Companion to American Military History*, Oxford, UK: Oxford University Press, 1999, pp. 683-686.

57. See Michael C. C. Adams, *Our Masters the Rebels: A Speculation on Union Military Failure in the East, 1861-1865*, Cambridge, MA: Harvard University Press, 1978.

58. See Patrick Porter, *Military Orientalism: Eastern War Through Western Eyes*, London, UK: C. Hurst, 2009, for intelligent discussion of this matter.

59. David Galula, *Counterinsurgency Warfare, Theory and Practice*, Westport, CT: Praeger Security International, 2006; Robert Thompson, *Defeating Communist Insurgency. The Lessons of Malaya and Vietnam*, New York: Frederick A. Praeger, 1966; and Kilcullen, *The Accidental Guerrilla.*

60. Antulio J. Echevarria II, *Challenging Tranformation's Cliches*, Carlisle, PA: Strategic Studies Institute, U.S. Army War College, December 2006, p. 23.

61. See David E. Johnson, *Learning Large Lessons: The Evolving Roles of Ground Power and Air Power in the Post-Cold War Era*, MG-405-AF, Santa Monica, CA: RAND, 2006. I discuss this topic in *Understanding Airpower: Bonfire of the Fallacies*, Maxwell AFB, AL: Air Force Research Institute, Air University Press, March 2009, pp. 31-35.

62. Derek Robinson, *Damned Good Show*, London, UK: Cassell, 2003, p. 302.

63. This erroneous thesis is slain convincingly in Richard K. Betts, "Is Strategy an Illusion?" *International Security*, Vol. 25, No. 2, Fall 2000, pp. 5-50.

64. Samuel P. Huntington, *The Soldier and the State: The Theory and Politics of Civil-Military Relations*, New York: Vintage Books, 1964.

Made in the USA
San Bernardino, CA
09 December 2013